Contact Center/Customer Service Excellence
Metrics that Matter!

Ray Roberge

ISBN:1515344142
ISBN-13: 978-1515344148

DEDICATION

This book is dedicated to my wife, Laurie, and my children, Taylor and Leslie. I appreciate their endless support and encouragement; without it, this book couldn't have been written.

CONTENTS

Acknowledgements

I would like to acknowledge the many contact center professionals that I have worked with who are committed to providing "World Class" customer service. We have spent many hours together resolving customer issues and creating long-term customer loyalty. Also a big thank you to Laurie and Darcie, who tried their best to turn a lot of ideas into something (hopefully) readable and understandable to you, the reader. Without the help of many, this book could not have been written.

1. WHY DO METRICS MATTER?

What's the big deal? You know your team is doing a fine job and your customers are happy, right? If your superiors ask how your team is doing, you quickly assure them that you are busy as ever.

The challenge you face is to actually measure "busy"? Is it a productive busy or a busywork busy? Is busy 10 calls per day or 75 calls per day? Is it 10 orders per hour or 10 orders per day? Do you measure orders by the line or by the order? How fast are you answering the phone and does it make a difference? Employees always say they are busy and don't know how they manage to get all their work done in a day. Very rarely will employees say that there is not enough work to do because that could eliminate their job.

How do you know when you need to add to your employee headcount or look into new technology to make your operation more efficient? How do you know if you are working efficiently if you don't measure it? Why would management care? They don't know what you do every day.

If you haven't heard it yet, you will: How do you know how you are doing if you don't measure it? What are the trends? What is World Class? Are you winning or losing the battle? You may think you are doing great, but your competitors may be beating you because they know what matters and they measure it. Even worse for you, they ask their customers how they are doing and they track that as well. In addition to measuring, they take action to improve their metrics to deliver even more value to the customer at the lowest cost.

Leaders know that their business needs to make a profit. If the profits are not on target, companies start to look at ways to eliminate cost to improve margins and increase operating income. The CEO may not be the expert in your particular area, but he or she knows what the operating expenses should be for the business. If they come looking for cost savings, you need to show the leaders that you are creating value for your customers at the lowest cost for the company.

I was a Regional Customer Service Manager in one business where I didn't have direct responsibility for the customer service and warranty teams because they were decentralized and they reported directly to each manufacturing plant.

We had just implemented a new phone system and were now measuring calls, call lengths, etc. One day while I was visiting a plant, the supervisor told me that he didn't believe the new phone reports shed any light on his department's efficiency. He felt that his team was well-managed and he was on top of all the activities in his department, but he needed more employees to handle the increased call volume.

I asked if he would run a few reports for me so I could review them. As I was reviewing the reports, I noticed that two of his employees made three times more outbound phone calls than the rest of the team. I thought this was odd since we were mainly an inbound call center.

When I met with the supervisor the next day to discuss my findings, he was perplexed. He stated that he would meet with his team to see what was happening.

Two weeks later, I received a call from the supervisor informing me that he had terminated one employee and put the second one on a written warning. He told me that the report had uncovered that these two employees were speed dialing the local radio station to play contests. They would call and hang up repeatedly to be the seventh caller. So I asked if he now thought the phone reports were going to be helpful in the long term.

He stated that he now believed the phone reports and would start to track the call activities more closely. Furthermore, he would not need additional people at this time to handle the call volume. This supervisor and I collaborated on a number of projects after this to make huge improvements at his facility.

In the following chapters, I will be discussing phone metrics because these tend to be the lifeblood of contact centers. You can keep metrics on many things, but make sure the metrics you record are meaningful, add value for your customer, and create actions if they are not where you want them to be. The resounding core of the major factors in a call center are:

1. Staffing and adjustments you can make.
2. Efficiency through technology.
3. Continuous improvement; never stop looking for a better way.

Do not waste your time tracking metrics if they will not produce improvement actions for the long term. Let's get started.

2. SERVICE LEVEL

Service level is one of the mainstay metrics of a call center. Service level is simply all the calls that your teams answer in 30 seconds or less. You may hear people refer to it as 90/30 (i.e. 90 % calls answered in 30 seconds). Divide the number of calls answered in 30 seconds by the number of total calls you took that day and you have your service level. This metric is key because customers do not like to wait for someone to answer their call.

It sounds easy, but accomplishing this is a challenge for many reasons. Let's look a little deeper.

Fortunately, these days most phone systems have the ability to run many reports for you. If you are not currently tracking service levels, check with your phone support representative to see if he or she can get the report run for you. If the representative doesn't know how, check with your phone system provider. If you have Automated Call Distribution (ACD) system, you should be able to pull this report through the phones reporting screens.

The Gold Standard for call service level is 90%. This means you answer 90% of your calls in 30 seconds or less. When this is reached consistently, it is known as "World Class" standards. Don't get discouraged if you are not there yet. . Trust me; you have to be very disciplined to achieve this service level on a consistent basis unless you have an army of people. Most companies do not have this abundance of manpower.

The next challenge is that your group doesn't only answer calls, but also has other tasks to accomplish to make the department function properly. You need to determine the best process to balance these tasks and still answer your customer calls.

First let's discuss the calls themselves.

1. Calls don't come in one at a time. They are random. Do you receive heavier call volume in the morning or afternoon? To

address this, you need to determine the heaviest call volume times so you can plan your staffing accordingly. You may need multiple shifts or staggered lunch breaks to make sure you have adequate coverage. Again, phone reports can be used to help determine the heavy volume times. Phone reports can give you call volume in 15 to 30 minute increments, which makes planning much easier.

2. Some calls are longer than others. You need to evaluate why these calls are long, and whether there is anything you can do to make them shorter. Is there information your agents need that should be more accessible? Can you provide the customer a document so they can help themselves? Is there information from other departments that can be added to your knowledge base to give your employees easy access to this information?

3. Calls are not all the same, so do you need to break them into different call queues? Determine whether your team can answer the questions or whether you'll need specialists in the particular area in question. It is easier to cover call volume when your team can handle all calls equally? If you have a large product line or something that is very technical, you may need to create separate queues for tracking reasons. You do not want to waste the customer's time by having people answer the phone that can't answer the question. If you have to create multiple queues, make sure it is easy for the customer to navigate your options (press 1 for customer service, press 2 for sales, etc.). Make sure the most popular options are listed first.

Let's look at the obvious challenge in service level percentage. Do you have enough people to answer calls, order products, check order status, and answer product questions? How do you determine that? Companies don't want to employ more people than necessary! It cuts into profits. The good news is there's help. The Erlang C formula was created to estimate how many people you need to answer phone calls. Look up Erlang C on the Internet and you will find a number of sites that guide you through this task.

If you are working to determine the staffing you need at an established center beyond the Erlang C formula, you can conduct a time study. Divide all the tasks your group has to accomplish by the total number of man-hours you have available. Theoretically, this will determine whether you have enough people or not.

Here are three things to review that could improve your service levels and possibly lessen the need for more staffing:

1. The phone system call reports give you the raw data for analysis so you can solve the service level challenge. Obviously not all companies have the option of hiring more people to address the service level, but there are a number of ways to improve your service level using the resources you already have. Consider technology to make your department more efficient. Computer Telephony Integration (CTI) software can make answering calls more efficient by identifying the caller. Meet with your IT team to investigate further.
2. Review your processes to see if there are things you can do to eliminate waste and free up personnel.
3. See if you can give your customers ways to get information themselves. This can be through your website or documents you can send them via email.

Dig into the data to improve your customer's experience. Help your employees create value for your company.

3. ABANDON RATE

Abandon rate is a straightforward metric. A call is abandoned when the customer is hanging up for whatever reason. There are a number of reasons why customers hang up, but you need to find out why so your business doesn't suffer. We will explore a number of these reasons.

The caller could have simply dialed the wrong number. This typically happens within the first 10 seconds of a call. The phone reports give the time duration before the call is abandoned. As a rule, it takes about 10 seconds for the phone to ring three times. I disregard abandoned calls within 10 seconds because I have found that the caller just dialed the wrong number or picked the wrong option. I only get concerned if there are a large number of calls within 10 seconds; otherwise, I subtract them from the total number of abandoned calls to calculate my abandonment rate for each department.

If you have a high service level, your abandoned rate call percentage should be very low. World Class standards are 2 to 4 percent abandonment rate.

When reviewing your abandon rate, pay attention to the length of time your customers are willing to hold before abandoning the call. If you are a business-to-business call center, your customers tend to hold longer because they need your help. Even in this scenario it is not acceptable to have high hold times, which we will discuss in the next chapter. If your customer is a dealer or an installer, they may get into the habit of hanging up and redialing quickly to see if they can catch an available representative. Unfortunately, this creates more inefficiency because it just puts them back at the end of the queue again, wasting the time of both parties.

Review the following tasks if you have high abandon rates:

1. Identify when the abandon calls are happening. If they are happening during a particular time of day, you may need to

adjust your staffing, especially during lunch or break times, to have better coverage.

2. Check the vacation schedule to make sure there are not too many employees off during the same time periods.

3. Hold training during off-peak times to allow for maximum coverage during the busy times.

4. If you are using an Automatic Call Distribution (ACD) routing make sure your most popular options are presented first so customers don't have to hold on the phone for a long time before being offered the selection they want. Also, announce changes to your call selections up front if you change your selections.

5. If all the above options are in order, you need to review your staffing to determine whether you have enough people. Time studies can be conducted to uncover tasks that are consuming your employees' time. Time studies are also helpful to uncover tasks that add little value to your operation.

6. Value Stream Map (VSM) some of your high-volume processes to see if waste can be eliminated. VSM is a method for analyzing the current state and designing an ideal state for a series of activities (for example: order entry process) that take a product or a service from its beginning to the customer. The goal is to identify time-wasting activities and eliminate them to gain efficiency and a superior customer experience. This will create higher efficiency and availability to attend to customer needs. I have personally seen efficiency gains of 75% or more in my departments. Shocking but true!

Service level and abandonment rates are directly related, so pay attention to both of them as you review your call metrics for improvement opportunities.

4. AVERAGE HOLD TIME VS. MAX DELAY TIME

I've seen companies base their performance on average hold time. This can lead you down a path to complacency, particularly if you have multiple skill queues. A low-volume queue with high hold times can be masked by a high-volume queue with much lower hold times. In the end the average looks acceptable, but some of your customers are not happy with your response times when calling into the low-volume high hold-time queue.

As a customer, I do not care what your average hold time is if I have to wait 20 minutes for someone to answer my call. This is where paying attention to your max delay calls is important. Max delay equals your calls that have the longest hold time. This could be one call during a busy time of the day or a series of calls with the same high hold time.

I recommend that you evaluate hold times in conjunction with service level. If you have a high service level, you should have very low hold times, giving you a very low average. In this instance, you should check out the max delay calls to ensure you are not leaving a few calls hanging out there. It's probably not a showstopper, but being the best at what you do involves continuous improvement to stay ahead of the competition.

If you have high hold times and/or high average hold times, your service level will suffer and your abandonment rate will be higher than you would like.

World Class standards state that your hold times should be 1½ minutes or less. Again, if your service level is World Class, all the other levels you measure are going to fall in line. You will only have to fine-tune things to get them in line if they are slightly out of tolerance.

If you have high hold times, you need to check the following items similar to the abandon rate in chapter 3.

1. Review the time of day where high hold times are occurring to see if you can adjust your staffing, training, or other activities that are taking people away from the phones.

2. Review all your skill queues to make sure there are not a small number of high hold time/max delay calls that may be overlooked because all other metrics are in line. This will help you catch a potential issue early before it gets worse.

You may want to create trend charts for your metrics so you can quickly take action if you start to see a downward trend or sequences of high variability. You can look at them individually, but also trend them together to see if they are in balance with each other.

If you see a spike in hold times, take the occurrence as an opportunity to find the root cause of the issue.

Drive continuous improvement! Your customers will love you for it.

5. AUXILIARY TIME

Auxiliary Time (aux time) selections are used in many different ways, but it really means that the representative is not available to take a call because he or she is engaged in another activity. The activity could be lunch, breaks, training, projects, etc.

It is up to the supervisor and/or manager of the department to determine how they use aux time selections. Using aux time selections for a myriad of different activities allows you to track how much time an individual representative is spending on any one activity. It is critical that you have goals for each activity to ensure the aux time is used effectively.

By using aux time selections in combination with how many calls a representative takes, you can monitor every minute that the representative is logged into the phone system. This is helpful to teams when adjustments need to be made to better serve the customer throughout the day.

Advantages of using aux time selections:

- It can be programmed into the phone system so standard reports can be run.
- It gives your representatives clear direction of how to utilize their time when not in an available state awaiting a customer call or interaction (for example: lunch, email, training, etc.)
- The report is a great tool to review with your employees to let them know how they are doing against the established departmental goals.

Disadvantages of using aux time selections:

- If you have too many selections, your employees may not use the selections correctly which will give you inaccurate reporting.
- If you don't review the aux time statistics on a regular basis, your employees will wonder why they have to use them to track their time.

Remember, the use of aux time selection reports are to assist you in making decisions about how to provide better service and value to the customer. Make sure what you are tracking is relevant to your operation. Engage your employees to review this item from time to time to ensure that your team sees value in the aux time selections.

6. PERCENT TIME AVAILABLE BY AGENT

This metric tells you how many minutes your representative is available to take a customer call. The goal is to have a good balance between all the representatives in your department. This metric is also a standard output from your phone system so it an easy report to run. So when would this metric be valuable?

It is valuable in the following situations:

- When you have multiple skills options that customers can select. If you don't have enough representatives trained for a particular skill option, it will create an unbalanced workload for your team. The Percent Time Available metric will identify this situation very quickly. The team that has the training for that skill will be taking more calls than the team that is not trained for that skill option.
- It can identify training opportunities to balance your skill options.
- If you have remote teams or third-party centers, it will identify whether you are using these sites effectively to create the best service for the customer.
- It can also identify representatives who are purposely holding back and letting their teammates answer the call first. Trust me, this does happen!

This metric is not a primary driver, but it can be used if your service levels start to dip. It is also very beneficial if you have multiple teams that are local and/or remote to make sure the skill option level is balanced. I have run into situations where a remote team has 30% more available hours than my local team. It identified that the remote site was experiencing high turnover and was not training the representatives on the right skill options. The local team was getting swamped with calls and the remote team was sitting waiting for the phone to ring. It allowed the managers to quickly take corrective action to improve the service to our customers.

7. EMAIL TURNAROUND TIME

More and more customers are communicating through email. They expect a consistent turnaround time when they place orders, ask technical questions, request an order status, etc.

World Class organizations strive to answer emails within 4 hours. The important idea here is to make sure your customer is aware that you will be answering the email in a reasonable amount of time. Follow-up calls to unanswered emails can be avoided by either sending an automated response or have a published turnaround time easily accessible to the customer. Turnaround time for answering emails can depend on the department being asked the question. For my groups, we try to return tech support emails in 1 hour or less, while customer service emails are answered within 4 hours. The goal is to do what you say you are going to do on a consistent basis to gain your customers trust and loyalty.

Make sure your sales team is aware of your goals for each team so they can be your advocate to the customer. These turnaround goals can be used for internal email traffic as well. My inside sales teams routinely need help from our tech support team. It makes my teams more efficient to send an email and know they will get an answer in an hour rather than having to get up and try to locate an available tech support representative. We all know when employees leave their desk you lose operational efficiency time and time again.

Tips for emails:

- Set goals for email turnaround and make sure your customers are aware of your response times.
- Use your sales team to communicate the news to their customers.
- Use the same goals for internal team communications.
- Consistency is key

8. ORDER ENTRY ACCURACY

This metric is critical to customer service or your order management group. I've always called my order entry/management group "Customer Service". They do much more than enter orders into the company's order management system, and I think you cheapen their value by labeling them "Order Management or Order Entry". That's my two cents on that one.

Order accuracy of 99% and above is World Class and needs to be as close to 100% as possible. Here's why: Every mistake, such as shipping the wrong product or wrong number of products costs extra time and work on the back side, such as issuing credits and additional shipping charges. It causes customer frustration and costs the company money. Think of this as the "Ease of Doing Business". Fewer mistakes are less costly to both the company and the customer.

Now let's look at order accuracy in terms of time. Every mistake takes a teammate away from completing productive work. Obviously teams do not like to keep going back to fix mistakes, so it is imperative that the order be entered correctly the first time. It also causes problems and frustration for the customer. When they receive the wrong product, it causes delays because the product doesn't match the purchase order. Then the rash of phone calls and emails ensues to get the issue resolved.

You should also look at how you can automate the order entry process as much as possible. You can use an Electronic Data Interface (EDI) or a web portal where customers can enter their own orders. This lets the system and the business rules established within the system cull out the mistakes. It puts your team in the position to deal with only the exceptions. If you are not using one of these techniques, I would encourage you to explore them because they can help your team become more productive.

Also look at ways to create a written standard operating procedure for the order entry process to give your team a standardized process to enter a correct order. This makes training new employees easier and also gives you a guide to do refresher training.

Customer service is the face of your company, so it is critical to give your customers a great up-front experience.

ORDER ENTRY ACCURACY CREATES A HAPPY AND LOYAL CUSTOMER! START MEASURING IT AND SEE THE DIFFERENCE.

9. CUSTOMER SATISFACTION (CSAT)/VOICE OF CUSTOMER (VOC)

We'll start with a simplistic way to measure customer satisfaction, mostly used before the Internet was widely used. Then we'll move to a more electronic method, which is mostly used today.

When I managed my first call center, it was 19 people strong and we took orders over the phone or received orders by mail. The center didn't measure anything. I knew this was not going to work long term so I started by measuring orders per person per day. In addition, I started recording customer complaints about product shortages and late shipments.

We averaged seven orders per day per person. The challenge was that in order to keep our distribution center efficient, we needed to keep the orders flowing with the least amount of people. My employees always said that they were very busy and could not do any more.

I challenged them to take nine orders per person per day and to improve our customers' experience. Needless to say, they were not happy and thought it couldn't be done. We started very simply by doing some problem solving. I asked my employees a question: What keeps us from completing orders when our customers call? There were a number of factors we quickly found that were occupying my customer service team. They were in fact busy, but for the wrong reasons. Product shortages from inaccurate inventory or damaged product were holding up the process. There was also a problem with incomplete customer or product information. We were spending too much time scheduling loads with the warehouse. Finally, the customer callbacks to rectify order issues were taking an exorbitant amount of time.

Needless to say, with a little work meeting with the different department managers, we found solutions to identifying product shortages early so we could fill the order in full, reducing customer callbacks.

To solve the incomplete customer data, we made a business rule that we would not enter an order unless we had all necessary information about the customer. We also gave our sales force an easy-to-use guide with information we would need for any of their orders.

I found that my team liked helping with load scheduling because it got them off the phone and gave them a break from putting in orders.

The above measures helped in reducing customer callbacks since there were far fewer order issues. In less than 2 months, we were up to nine orders per day per person and my team was happier because they did not have to deal with daily delays from the issues mentioned above. Customer complaints changed to positive comments from our customers.

Our customers were much happier because they were getting their orders on time and correct. This was a simple but effective way to increase customer satisfaction.

Now let's get some feedback from the customer by asking them how you are doing. Voice Of Customer (VOC) can be done in several ways:

1. A once-a-year survey with 25 to 50 questions. However, it is difficult to get a high response rate on this survey because it takes quite a bit of time to complete.

2. Many companies are now using the Net Promoter Score (NPS) to see how they are doing. It starts with what is called the money question: "Would you refer us to a friend or colleague?" This works well, but it is a bigger financial investment to get it completed. Most companies hire a third-party firm to administer the survey and tabulate the results, which requires a significant financial investment.

3. If you send out follow-up emails from your customer interactions, you can attach a survey to the email for the customer

to complete. Surveys are usually five questions or less, and you can use the "money question" to get an unofficial net promoter score.

I prefer to use the third option to get immediate feedback on my teams. First, you get a large number of responses so you get a great sample size across your customer base. It also gives you feedback of your performance within hours or days of the interaction so you can take corrective action if needed. You can also catch your employees doing things right by reviewing the positive comments from your customers. We post customers' positive comments in each department to recognize our employees' accomplishments.

My current company still does an NPS once a year to have a recognized VOC measurement. I compare the NPS responses with our departmental VOC responses to address any gaps we may have between the two data collection methods. This is a great litmus test to make sure you are aligned.

The most important advice I can give you is to regularly review this data. It will help you create a long-term competitive advantage with your customers. Customers are not bashful; they will tell you how they are feeling, whether it is good or bad.

10. WRAP UP

Let's wrap things up. There are numerous ways to measure call center performance, or your department's performance overall. I have reviewed the main reporting methods in most centers. If you have a unique situation that needs additional measurement, by all means keep track of it. Just make sure what you are measuring is relevant, and if it needs improvement, you can take action to improve the metric. Far too often I have seen companies running metrics that have no bearing on creating customer value.

Make sure you are measuring what matters to the customer and gives them an overall better experience with your company. If it doesn't matter to the customer, you have to determine why you are keeping the metric and what value it provides to your team.

Meet with your teams on a regular basis to review the metrics and ensure they understand its importance and the role they play to keep it above the goal. If your teams don't understand the metric, it will be difficult to sustain them over time. Ask for their input to keep them engaged and get the most out of what you are measuring. Actively ask for their continuous improvement ideas. You will be amazed by their creativity.

I would recommend sharing your metrics with your sales team and other departments. They can offer input and give you feedback from the customer to make sure you are hitting on all the important areas that customers care about.

Good luck in creating a "World Class" call center.

ABOUT THE AUTHOR

Ray Roberge is a Customer Service professional who has led "World Class" contact centers and has been recognized for creating first class customer service, warranty and technical support teams for a number of Fortune 100 companies.

He holds an MBA from the University of Tennessee and has more than 20 years of Customer Service experience in multiple industries.

www.ingramcontent.com/pod-product-compliance
Lightning Source LLC
Chambersburg PA
CBHW070756180526
45168CB00004B/1631